Whale-shocked

Sue Aldred

Whale-shocked

A family story in verse

Acknowledgements

My sincere thanks to the following people for making this work possible: my writing group, Literary Optimists, for all their encouragement and feedback, with a special mention to Karen Throssell, our wonderful tutor. To Stephen Lyons, whose incomparable genealogical research sent me on this journey. Michael, your loving support and patient assistance is, as always, much appreciated. To all my dear family, without whom this story would not have been told.

Whale-shocked: A family story in verse
ISBN 978 1 76109 453 8
Copyright © text Sue Aldred 2022
Cover image: Whale fluke, iStock 156056693, Jeff Thompson

First published 2022 by
GINNINDERRA PRESS
PO Box 3461 Port Adelaide 5015
www.ginninderrapress.com.au

Contents

Introduction	7
Beginnings: Cruden Bay	9
John Mackie	11
Charlet Leask	12
Peterhead	13
Bairns #1	16
Bairns #2	17
David Leask	18
The Foy	20
The Eclipse: Captain David Gray	21
Captain David Gray reflects	24
To Shetland	25
The unknown north	26
First iceberg	27
The harpooner	29
The flensing	31
Back to port	33
Keith Inch	34
Bowhead whales and whaling	36
The whale speaks	37
John Mackie speaks	40
The 20th century	43
Family holidays #1	44
Family holidays #2	45
Family holidays #3	47
Covid #1	49
Covid #2	50
Covid #3	52
References	53

Introduction

In 2019, I was settling my late mother's affairs in the UK. Going through her papers, I was again reminded of how little I knew about my family history. A friend and avid genealogist, Stephen Lyons, offered to do some research. While he could only find out a little about my family, he struck gold with an ancestor of my husband's. John Mackie, born in Cruden, Scotland, had gone to sea as a ship's cook on the whaling vessel *Eclipse* in the 1800s. What a story. Reflecting further, I recognised how whales formed a thread through our family from the 1860s to the present day. I'm sure this is common in many families, given the ubiquitous nature of whaling products in use worldwide and the attention given to whales in the 1970s at the start of the environmental movement.

I tried writing in prose but it came across as wooden, so I pursued long-form poetry as an alternative. It is a work of creative non-fiction (CNF). As in all CNF, I have attributed values and emotions to John that may well not be accurate; however, observing his descendants leads me to suspect I am close to the truth.

Covid 19 has prevented me from visiting most of the places mentioned here, but I look forward to doing so in the future.

Beginnings: Cruden Bay

57.4181° N, 1.8508° W

Offshore, in cold grey North Sea,
whale spouts, rolls, breaches –
heading due north, ancient
ancestral trajectory,
bound to travel

Dark beady eyes gaze
whale sees man, man sees whale,
seeing yet unknowing.
Whale calls, sets course north
journeys, stories, songs
weave whale and human

Undulating dunes, pale pink sand
lapped by chill waves.
Fifty-seven degrees north, facing east,
bathed in pale Scottish light…
next stop Scandinavia.

The ancients laid their dead
here, in this cairn,
Catto Long Barrow.
King Malcolm left his mark
killed invaders on soft pink sand
Croch Dain: Dane slaughter

Slains Castle wrought in stone,
high on cliff. Fine, baronial mansion
reimagined by the eighteenth Earl,
fanciful, octagonal rooms.
Visited by Bram, inspiring
Dracula…

Cruden – simple town,
parish school, kirk,
towering episcopal church.
Two hundred years on
fisher-houses cling to harbour
pastels soften once forbidding granite

Here John Mackie was born,
shoemaker, cook, whaler.
Ancestor.

John Mackie

Bachelor of this parish*

I gang ten mile tae Peterhead, Broad Street,
for the market tae sell ma shoes
feeing market† this, mebbe new work for me
a change frae makin' of the shoes

I first saw her there, roundin' yon corner,
clad in hues of country – grey, moss green,
simple clothes, hand-woven, knitted.
Bonny and blithe skipped she,
wi' her group o' quines – all o' the land.
Skirts flyin' in the wind, shawls pulled tight agin
north sea howl. Stout boots, clean aprons
bright hair, bright laughter

Aye, I were weak at the knees
stupid grin acrass ma face
she picked up ma shoes

---

* This is a nod to Doric Scots, which would have been spoken by John and his family. Doric refers to the Scots language as spoken in the north-east of Scotland and comes from the Greek for rural, rustic or 'of the land'.
† A 'feeing' market, held weekly each Friday, acted like an employment exchange.

Charlet Leask

Spinster of this parish

I love Friday market, time tae talk wi'
ma friends and eat a bowl of brose.
Aye, though yon smells – herring curing,
kelp drying, fair brings tears tae ya een.

Da died awae fishin' silver darlings,
Ma brought me here as a wee bairn.
Such change I seed, less weavin' o' the wool
more twistin o' rope, ship-building all over.

Peterhead. Still our Blootoon,
me a bloomogganner
at the market. There I first met John,
up frae the country, Cruden.
'Hurry along, lassie' said the crones
'22 years ye are now.
Nae husband means nae bairns,
that means nae life.'

Peterhead has been a fishing port on the NE coast of Scotland since 1380 and is named after a twelfth-century church on the headland dedicated to St Peter (the fisher of men). Known by locals as the 'Blootoon' or Blue Town, Peterhead locals derived their name of bloomogganner from the blue (bloo) worsted stockings (moggins) worn by fishermen. Local industry included a brewery, brickworks, dyeworks, a carding and spinning mill for wool. Sea kelp was gathered for manure and cattle feed. By 1850 the traditional industries were disappearing, with ship-building and rope-making dominating.

Peterhead

57.5081° N, 1.7841° W

Leaving Cruden for marriage, for Charlet,
John absorbs Peterhead's voice.
Trudges its streets, fishes its waters
grows his family

The voice of the Blootoon
so unlike his pink, sandy bay home.
Tones harsher, louder
confront him, make him smaller…
…no denying, though, Blootoon
gives shelter for his Mackie brood
all nine of them, all their lives

John listens to her story.
Seven hundred years ago
named for St Peter, fisher of men,
headland church bears saint's name.
Fisherfolk flocked here for silver darling.
Hundreds on hundreds of boats…
…thousands on thousands of workers

Blue, bloo granite blocks made them homes,
blue, bloo fisher folk's stockings – moggins –
made them Bloomogganners

She grew and prospered, spreading her streets'
capacious skirts, gathering folk in.
They brewed beer, made bricks, spun wool,
gathered kelp. Drank, fought, married,
lived, loved, died.
Things changed when the whaling came…

…she grew great, a premier port,
whale oil, whale bone, whale smell,
boiled-up blubber, broken-down bone.
Exports, imports, riches,
money, mansions, new gentry
culture, schools, libraries.
Associations for Science and the Arts!

Long after John departs, the whaling's gone.
Peterhead still lives oil, deep-sucked from sea.
Refuge from North Sea storms remains,
her sheltering, easterly, harbour.

Peterhead became a leading whaling port in the UK with its population growing to around 6,000. The harbour, originally developed in 1587, began to expand and prosper as a port in the seventeenth and eighteenth centuries, with an expansion of the herring or 'silver darlings' fleet. There were 800 herring boats in 1855, employing around 7,000 people across the industry. Trading of cured herring and, later, whale, seal and granite gave Peterhead a thriving export trade. Its position as the most easterly port that could be reached by vessels from the north of Europe hit by storms in the North Sea made Peterhead an important refuge. Peterhead boasted a parish school, a public library and a Mechanics' Library as well as an Association for Science and the Arts giving weekly lectures. There were also hot and cold public baths!

John, and Charlet (Charlotte) met at the Peterhead market in May and were married in September 1858. They went on to have seven children:

Elizabeth	b 1858
John	b 1861
William	b 1863
Charlotte	b 1865
Maggie	b 1868
Jane	b 1871
Minnie	b 1874

They lived in Peterhead all their married lives. John became a seaman, probably starting out on the herring boats. They moved from Back Gate to Long Gate and finally to Jamaica Street, this last a tied cottage linked to the wealthy ship-owning and whaling family, the Grays.

Bairns #1

Charlet

Familiar pangs, here comes another, number five.
Pop them out like shelling peas –
hardly need the howdie now,
pains, smell, sweat, final slithering push.
Another girl! Born behind
a curtain, other bairns in the next room,
lit by smoking, stinking whale oil lamp.

We need to get out of here
out of this wee house of cold, dark granite.
Back Gate? Long Gate? All the same to me,
just bairns underfoot, not enough food…
hard feeding mouths when work's not paying.
Time to put the pressure on.
Get that brother o' mine
tae talk some sense into John.

Bairns/birth: Scotland was a leader in the registration and training of midwives, largely thanks to (the rather regrettably named) Doctor William Smellie, known as the 'father of British midwives'. Controversially, for the times, he started his career as a male midwife, becoming a doctor in 1745. In north-eastern Scotland, midwives were colloquially known as a skilly, a handywoman or a howdie. She would often stay with the family for a couple of days after the birth, helping with the laundry and the new mother. Large towns at that time boasted lying-in hospitals for births and lying-in, but most women still delivered at home with a trusted midwife.

Bairns #2

John

Some complain about their bairns
me, I love, welcome, each one –
never thought there'd be five in ten years.
Provider, protector, father – these are heavy burdens,
yet lightly borne for love of Charlet

David Leask

Charlet's brother recruits John – ship's cook

Brother-in-law, it's time tae make some real money!
Couple o' turns on the whalers and your pockets will be full.
Ye'll nae have to kill the beasts, just feed the men,
cook their dinner, boil their water…
…right fug below deck, mind ye,
tobacco smoke, too many bodies, lots of grog…
but some fine Shetland fiddle to be heard.

Cap'n Gray's a bit of a snob, trails friends along,
educated types, observers, artists.
Then ye'll need tae cook sea fowl, crack out red wine
for thaim to drink at thair cards.
One voyage's wage is enough to set ye up for life.
Get down the port, sign your name, ye'll nae regret it,
adventure…
…so John did…

…proof exists in faded monochrome,
he stands tall, staring through time
in thick padded jacket, right hand clutching lapel,
left buried deep in pocket.
He wears a weskit, collarless shirt,
cloth cap with leather peak
set at jaunty angle, shading right eye.
Surrounded by crew, no smile,
rather puzzlement, faint perturbation.
What am I doing here?

The Foy

All around the old port,
taverns, inns, alight, abuzz, packed tight,
warm refuge from January frost and snow.
Captains kit crew with woollen mitts, guernseys, scarves, caps,
shipowners pockets turned inside out
paying men off with the Foy, grand, drunken party,
promise of fortune, good times, wealth for all.
John, family man, sober man – bemused at wild frivolity –
ship's cook? The *Eclipse*?
It seems so.

Men dance around him, sing, play fiddle, eat, drink.
There'll be scant cause for a party in hard months to come.

Family, wives and lovers garland ships with ribbons, bows,
to bring their sea-set, north-bound, ice-pledged men luck.
John sees Charlet, his bairns, down on the dockside.
Through mist they float, unreal.

Sound the ship's horn! Stand along the stern, boys,
wave farewell, catch favours and tokens…
…oranges, herrings, pennies thrown by beloveds.
Give three cheers as we ease out of port!
Then anchors down, to sleep off the grog…

The Foy was an event for signing up and kitting out the crew, as well as a rowdy party. It was funded by the shipowner prior to the season. When the ship sailed, it would be the last time the crew would see their wives and families until late summer or early autumn. During that period nothing would be heard of the ship or its crew.

The Eclipse: **Captain David Gray**

Aberdeen, 57.1497° N, 2.0943° W

Puffed-out pigeon chest he struts, David the younger –
now shipowner – Gray.
Look up to us Gray brothers now
we are whalers, three generations strong –
call me Prince of Whalers.

David, dockside, extols her virtues, the SS *Eclipse*.
His *Eclipse*.
Dark mutterings…surely bad omen
is the name not a curse on the ship?

But no, shouts Gray – innovation, excellence, wonder!
Eclipse is launched on the eclipse,
dignitaries all present.

Never before was a steamship like her –
see her strong hull, made of ironbark wood
all the way from Australia.
She has icebeams, iron plates, an oaken rudder
three-pling reinforcement, sixty-nine horsepower engines.
Painted black and white like her sister, *Hope*.
Her crew will number fifty-five fit men,
some frae the Blootoon, new hands and old.
Harpooners, spectioneers, ship's cook –
new man – John Mackie.

Eclipse's eight whaling boats dangle from davits
jaunty lilac, winsome white.
With these we chase the whales,
boast braw harpoons – Greener's guns.
Exploding heads, vertical planes,
guaranteed to pin the whale.
Iron tanks below to take the blubber…
…all up, twelve thousand pounds we spent.

January 1867…Aberdeen.
Eclipse breaks free of her moorings, sets sail
up to Peterhead, ready for the Season,
in search of the Greenland whale,
the right whale, the bowhead whale.
We'll make money, real money.

June

Saturday 5th light wind & clear
at 2 A.M. a Fish seen in the hole, at
half past 2 A.M. Alx Watt got
fast her but after having two
lines out, they got foul & nearly
took the Boat down, some of
the crew jumped in, the harpoon
came out & lost the fish —
at 10.A.M. Jas Summers got
fast a fish but the Harpoon drew out.

6 feet 6 in — at ½ past 10 Mr Foss got
fast a fish & got her dead
and at 11 A.M. G. Thomson
5 feet. 10 in — got fast another fish & got
her dead. at 2 P.M. had
both fish alongside the ship
at 3 P.M. commenced flenching and
finished at 10 P.M. No more fish
seen after 11 A.M. the seven ships
close beset

Captain David Gray reflects

'the captains belonged to a society which believed that the purpose of "nature"…was to provide for man's needs' – Duncan, p. 197

The whaling's been good to me
I own property, command respect,
crew live in tied cottages along Jamaica Street
landed gentry speak to me now.
I built me a grand mansion…aye!
Up on the Links, with the posh folk.

I followed voyages of early whalers,
shudder at the memory of *The Dee* in 1837, held fast by ice.
Crew suffering frostbite, scurvy, dying in the white, cold north.
Thirty-seven unmarked graves.

True, years ago, whale numbers were prodigious –
counted in hundreds, they are falling now.
Fewer beasts these days.
Well, there are always seals – prized white fur, clubbing easy.

Dinnae fret, ma boys, ma crew,
there is wealth enough for us.
We'll go further, further north than ever before,
80 degrees north.
The ice pack of Greenland calls.

To Shetland

59.8691° N, 1.2871° W

'…ship strong, crew healthy, ice open and fish plenty' – whaler's toast, Duncan p. 201

John shudders – *Eclipse* takes life, sails full, thrumming,
they have the northerly; wide grey sea, land fading to mist.
First stop Bressay Sound, pick up wild Shetland crew
there are Leasks, Leisks – Charlet's kin
yet seeming foreign in speech

Years of running frae press gangs, nae to fight
for southern kings in southern ships.
The customs men searched long and hard –
like otters were the Shetlanders,
fast, lithe, gone, with their booty.
Now they are thralled to new gentry –
crew their ships, drink their rum,
kill their whales, line their pockets.

The unknown north

After Shetland, all is new. Far beyond his known world,
three clear days in forty, smothering fog and snow
create new, swirling, misted worlds.
Sou'westerly gales hound them,
Eclipse's very bones creak in crushing ice.
Destruction all around, skinned seals lie rotting, wasted, spent,
mirages appear, ghost ships float above the horizon.
North, ever north!
The sun is here at midnight
the cold is the coldest ever known
eyelashes freeze, snap, tears gel, glued to cheeks.
What hell is this?

First iceberg

40-80° N

The ice was here, the ice was there,
The ice was all around:
It cracked and growled, and roared and howled,
Like noises in a swound!
– Coleridge

North of forty degrees
we keep extra watch
for icebergs

Bigger than a kirk they say
cold, glittering, blue, green
the part we see

They breathe wafts of
rotten ice stench exhaled by
ancient long-dead creatures

Icebergs speak,
emit noise,
creak, groan, shriek, sough, sigh

Ice favours us with a dock,
hems us in
sets fast around if we are still

Jigsaw floes on moving water
white griddle cakes in blue-green pan
Moving
        ever
                more
                        slowly –
                                – Icebound!

Ice that crushes ships' bows
lifts up sterns
ice thicker than the tallest crew

Rigging frozen with
transparent ice, like glass,
groaning, top-heavy

Ice – becomes a playground for some
Not us, not crew. Just
Captain, surgeon and the like,

hunt, just for sport,
mighty white northern bears,
shadows, spirits of the ice
left dead, abandoned.

The harpooner

60-75° N

'A fall, a fall', the cry goes up
we run, stumble and tip into our whale boat –
number six of eight,
jaunty lilac, winsome white… *Quick!*
whoever's first gets the prize.

Row quietly, boys, sneak up from behind
to the side…that's it…now – bump him!
The beast takes fright, back arches,
that's our target –
one shot of the harpoon penetrates tight skin,
cruel claws grip. That's enough to wing the beast –
run the line out…

…miles of line, smoking 'round the bollard
Wet her down, wet her down,
or we'll all be afire
Now the other boats join us, six harrying thrashing whale.
Look out for its tail!
Murderous brutes, wicked whales.

Harpooned whale hits boat, almost pitches crew
deep, deep in icy water…but no.
Dangerous, difficult – these whales need
exploding harpoons…boom!

Hours pass, we are far from *Eclipse*, but then,
look boys, he's tiring now!
Another lance, another stab, blood spouts from blowhole
that's it, he's floating, belly up.

A day's hard rowing now back to the mother ship,
to *Eclipse*.
Chain him up to the sides, work's not done yet.

The harpooner: whalers usually carried four or five harpooners, one of whom acted as the mate, or second-in-command. One harpoon boat would be launched on sighting the whale and, once a harpoon was successfully embedded in the whale, the other boats would follow from the whaling vessel, assisting with the hunt and often travelling miles from the mother ship.

The flensing

And so he comes to rest.
Bumping larboard, held with chains,
ropes, around the tail, head sternwards.
Fit blocks and pulleys, use tackle to pull
mighty head away from tail…
stretch him out, boys.

All crew on deck now, *Eclipse* moored, safe in ice-dock
ice holds her steady, sails furled, while we work.
*Cook! Bring a meal, we'll take a wee dram
afore labour begins*…the flensing.

John stalls, the sight of this first capture
riveted in his sight, his soul…
so huge, so black, so dead, trussed.
Awaiting
dis / mem / ber / ment.

Quaking, he approaches stinking crewmates
clutching bottle of Dutch courage…for him?
Or for exhausted harpooners
who play new roles now, shod with crampons,
clambering obscenely over the huge carcass.

Take care lads, there's skill involved…
wield yon blubber spade, haul belly jelly on deck.
Like so many ants, crew attack their booty –
chop, slice into cubes, throw down to black hold.
John never signed up for this.

Turn him over boys, strip away back fat,
then split his lips for the whalebone.
Then we're done – thirty ton of blubber
all in three hour.
Cook! Bring more food, for we hunger now.
White bears and sharks hunger too,
we leave them our mess,
our *kreng*.
No use to us.

John goes below
thoughts of food
repellent, obscene.

The flensing: many terms in whaling come from Dutch. Flensing, removal of the whale's blubber or flens-gut. The spektioneer oversaw the flensing process. Skeeman oversaw the crew, Krengers, who removed muscle. Crang or kreng was the term used to describe the 'waste' – discarded portions of the carcass left over after the baleen and blubber had been harvested. The whale meat was not eaten and left to rot on the ice.

Back to port

Ice closing over, time for home, family, lovers
all have waited long months.
A good season, this one,
fifteen whales taken,
profit guaranteed, easier life to come

Aye, ponders John
but this is a young man's work
my bones ache now
hands are scarred, blistered
face seared by icy wind

Sick I am of rancid cheese, salt beef and biscuit –
warm butter-rich burgoo
but a distant memory.

Through endless sea, ice,
mountains of waves, wind,
Eclipse and crew sail, stumble, pick
clinging to frigid northern coasts
Davis Strait, Baffin Bay,
always looking east
for Scotland's fair shore.

Burgoo is a seafarer's dish. The name has its origins in the Royal and Merchant Navies. While it can be a rich stew of meat and vegetables, the term can also be used for porridge, probably the case here.

Keith Inch

57.5000° N, 1.7667° W

Archways, alleys, doors, all
framed by whales' jawbones
erected by killer men
sign of their dominion

John views a hellish scene –
another trial before greeting loved ones.
It's all hands to dock at Keith Inch,
all hands on deck, unload the cargo –
Yes, even the cook.

Stench enough to knock you sideways
thick in the air, tangible,
fills eyes, nose, throat, hair
fills John's very being.

Ten-ton copper pots, furnace beneath
bubbling away day and night,
boiling that blubber down to oil,
channelled, steaming, white,
against cool northern sky.

Unload our blubber ready for the inchers
to stir with wooden poles.
Work not done yet, still the whalebone waits:
six hundred plates per beast, fifteen feet long.
Unload, and let the scrubbers do their work
hack away bone and gum, split into chunks.

Awae hame now, lads.
John reels, staggers, falls, mind whale-full,
whale-shocked.

Keith Inch: island off Peterhead, ironically now a terminal for North Sea oil rather than whale oil.

Bowhead whales and whaling

'People of the nineteenth century – across an array of classes, professions and life stages – dressed in, slept, and dreamt on the stuff of whales; they cooked with, played with, desired with and made art from, looked through, healed with, explored via, were disciplined by, disciplined with and made divinations out of whales. In the ordinary course of life, they were almost constantly in contact with whale-gleaned products, in much the same way as most people are never far from plastic objects… those nineteenth century forebears lived inside a whale-furnished world.' – Giggs, R., p. 43

One of the world's largest mammals, the bowhead whale can reach twenty metres in length and live for up to two hundred years. Its huge head forms one-third of its body, enabling it to break through sixty centimetres of Arctic ice. It has paired blowholes which can spout six metres high. Unusually, the bowhead has no dorsal fin. Its baleen plates, which act as filters for its feeding, measure four metres in length. It can remain underwater for up to one hour and it travels alone or in pods of up to six. It has the thickest blubber of any animal, up to fifty centimetres thick. This wealth of baleen and blubber led to merciless hunting.

Whaling was a controversial but vital element of the Scottish economy. It was vital to the jute industry – jute was soaked in whale oil to make it possible to spin.

The first use for whale oil was lamps and candles. As Scotland industrialised, it became widely used for sailmaking, processing woollen cloth, tanning, soap-making and metalworking. Whalebone, or baleen, is made of keratin, like fingernails and hair. It was highly valued for its flexible yet strong properties.

A bowhead whale found in 2007 had a harpoon head dated between 1885 and 1895 embedded in its head, putting its estimated age at well over a hundred years.

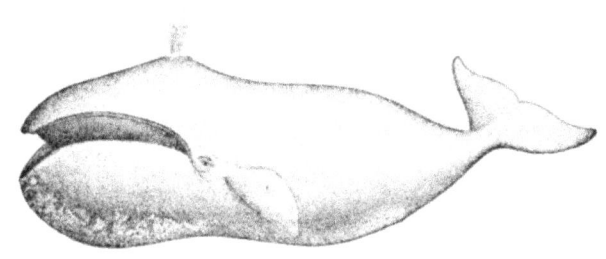

The whale speaks

Leviathan
Balaena mysticetus
Bowhead, one of a kind.
And right

in the sky
as Cetus, Greek sea monster
in wondrous stars —Mira, and
Diphda, orange-hued, this tail

cruising shallow Arctic seas
giant mouth gaping,
downcurved curtains of baleen
sift for sustenance.

Dark-bodied, strong-headed,
black velvet and sandpaper.
Small brown eyes, huge head.
Through Greenland pack ice
with pointed blowhole
spout high to vaulted sky

Hundreds of whale songs guide us
under the ice that hides us.
Love songs too –
if only you would listen
our calls unite us, bind us

Mother whale
ten years old
grows her baby
fourteen long months.
Minutes after birth it swims,
weighing two thousand pounds
dwarfing your puny harpoon boat
if only you would look.

And yes, we feel pain,
sandpaper skin tissue-thin.
Bird's footfall awakens our
slumber at pack-ice edge.
You do not hear or feel us,
merely see and hunt us…

…the cry goes up, boats are launched.
you fire weapons, armed with
claws, explosives.
Desperately we dive to ocean floor
seeking refuge…
…only to be dragged,
hauled back to you, on
thousands of yards of line
to be stabbed, hacked, mauled
to our deaths.

And for what?
You call me the right whale as
I float after death.
My blubber is thick
it makes oil to light your way,
to grease your machines
it makes the sails that drive
the very ships that kill me
it greases your ropes –
the very ropes that bind me.

My bone, my baleen
is precious too –
for fickle fashions,
narrow waists,
umbrellas to protect you
from the elements.
You use my bone to whip your horses
to weave your baskets
to scratch your backs.

You are our enemy,
carving us into component parts
leaving us.
Crang.

We will swim and sing again
but never forget.

John Mackie speaks

I am, I was,
shoemaker, fisherman, husband, father.
Craved domesticity, safety, yet
I became
ship's cook, SS *Eclipse*.

I saw, I felt,
conflict, fear, horror
beauty, wonder, loss
so far north, away from home, family.

I breathed
numinous, glass-clear air in
a land of fables, of strange peoples.

I gazed on
vistas of miles, across calm bays,
pellucid ocean, seabirds, silence.
Mountains etched on peerless blue sky,
marble glaciers, deep, dark turquoise-green sea,
mists, drifting, fine snow.

I heard
a thousand birds sing past on the wind
abundant life, bear, walrus –
whales spouting steamy geysers
calling, singing, dying

Amongst such beauty
men slaughter for wealth
there is no night, sleep snatched on deck
always waiting for the cry *'fall'*
then running, tumbling into boats

I wonder
where lies compassion, pity?
Sail past icy kills, putrid stench,
wanton waste, cruel carnage.
Predators screech and feast
scene from an icy hell

I list
supplies to support slaughter –
they appear mundane, innocent.
Salt beef, pork, cheese, butter,
sugar, tea, lime juice, suet…
…and, of course, grog.
All these keep the crew fit,
fit for foul, filthy work.

Brother-in-law lied to me
I worked the deck, saw, smelt metal blood
I moved the blubber, blubbered myself.
Whales are blubber, bone,
wealth, profit, commodity.
Yet I have seen them blow,
swim with calves, heard their songs
I feel their spirit haunting me

Six months is all it takes, he said –
six months for a year's wages
six months of hell
six months to undo your mind.

John Mackie: b. Cruden Bay, 1838, d. Peterhead, 1920.

    Modern-day sensibilities lead one to imagine that, for many men, the bloody horror that was whaling would haunt them all their lives. The sheer scale of the slaughter alone is unthinkable, coupled with months of isolation from home and family, forced into the company of strangers on crowded decks, exposed to brutal weather and dangerous seas – I think these days we would diagnose PTSD. Even the rewards might not have been enough. I find it significant that John listed his occupation as shoemaker when he married and seaman in the intervening years but reverted to shoemaker at his death. I like to think it is because he wanted no further truck with that brutal industry.

The 20th century

Ypres, 1917, 50.8492° N, 2.8779° E

Flanders Fields; man crouches, quivers
John's descendant, lost in swirling, choking gas
at Ypres. Half a million dead.

Survivors ever pounded by ghost bombs
in their heads. Twitching, groaning,
back in Blighty, while wives watch.

Worldwide carnage, in part, fuelled by whales.
Their oil, manhandled, made war's explosives.
Bowhead bounty now ravages, ruins
successors of the whale slaughterers.

Family holidays #1

Portsmouth, 1980s, 50.8198° N, 1.0880° W
John's descendants – great-great-grandson and wife (the author) and
three great-great-great-grandchildren (author's family)

'Whales are the common heritage of mankind' – UN, 1972
'Whales are an icon of no nation, but the planet at large' – Giggs, p. 63

Sun shines, boats bob, happy family waits for ferry,
big blue and white boat. Off to see the world…
…well, France anyway.

A floating rainbow! shout the children
*Greenpeac*e in port, back from chasing
those who would kill whales

Whales still dying, man still murdering
false science now sailing in
lethal factory ships

In Aldred kitchen hangs a poster –
all the whales of the world, colours, shapes, sizes.
So few still exist…

Whales sing us to sleep on C90 cassettes
mysterious songs from the deep.
Whale songs, world's songs…

Family holidays #2

Hervey Bay, 1993, 25.2882° S, 152.7677° E
John's great-great-granddaughter and author

Another boat bobs
Off Queensland's shore –
cruises, for whale-watching

We head far out, further than imagined.
There is a swell, we are green, queasy,
no breakfast, thanks…

In settling swell, we are told to look,
inexplicably, for footprints. And then
far off, a flattening on sea's surface…

…an almost-space where something should be.
A massive being, as long as our boat,
swims closer for a look at the humans.

Dark, beady eye exposed as whale turns,
floats on its side, sighs, whooshes,
sinks beneath us

only to rise again, other side –
(we don't know port from starboard)
We are transfixed, tearful, overwhelmed

A fin extends, flops back, looking lazy,
yet there is a huge wave.
It rocks us, we laugh, nervously

Humpback whales, here for birthing
in safe, shallow waters of the bay
They travel far, so far

Rocking silently on the glassy sea
we scan, whisper, watch.
A breach – the whale
throws its huge bulk out of the water

I swear I can hear it
yelling, wheeeeeee look at meeeeee…
…splash? Inadequate!
Small tidal wave…

It is joyous, moving. We can barely speak,
don't want to break the spell.
The whale watches us, keeps us company

for hours. And then it is gone, away
on mysterious missions. We drift shorewards
humbled, awed, silenced

Another boatload transformed,
converted. Spread the word! Protect whales!
They feel, like us, nurse their babies, like us

Whale as spiritual guide? Modern-day religion?
Sentient being, singer of songs…
speak to us, show us the way,
help us help ourselves…

Family holidays #3

Great Australian Bight, 2012 35.7696° S, 131.2809° E
John's youngest great-great-great-granddaughter and author

Black road-ribbon, lower edge of continental map,
here are John's descendants,
road-tripping, journeying, Perth to Melbourne

Rust-brown tourist sign – Great Australian Bight.
Shall we? Or not? Go on then.
We turn due south

A tourist centre, we are asked to pay
to see the whales. We're shocked!
Tell you what, says okker bloke,
go and have a look, if you don't see any
you don't have to pay.

The Bight is not the grey, forbidding world
we anticipated. It is bright turquoise, white,
cobalt sky above.
Late September, long walk to the sea,
wind breathes icy breath
straight off the Southern Ocean.
We shiver, huddle, descend,
reading information along the way

Don't go near the edge, I say
and she does
then we take silly pictures.
Further still, along the boardwalk
we reach the ocean's edge

Below us a miracle of southern right whales,
cousins of bowheads hunted by ancestor John.
They drift and wallow. Each, it seems, has a calf.

Is it real? Or can we hear them singing?
Ridiculously close, wallowing below us
aimless, sun-kissed. Are they happy,
rocking gently on the swell? We count…on and on…

Covid #1

London, 2020, 51.5074° N, 0.1278° W
John's oldest great-great-great-granddaughter

'Whales accrue pollution and industrial residue' – Giggs, pp. 305, 186

She sits at home in these plague times
writing China Dialogue, of whales,
of flocculent plumes.

John's descendant always loved nature,
could tell you all about a blue whale.
Now she reports that
science has discovered whale ecoservices –
(still focused on what they can do for us)

We continue to wreck the seas
and ruin the planet…a century of whaling
is like burning seven million rainforests –
coal-oil-based plastics wreak whale havoc.

Covid #2

St Andrews, Australia, 2020/21, 37.5920° S, 145.2812° E
John's great-great-granddaughter-in-law (author)

'A whale's whole body is its speaker' – Giggs, pp. 305, 186

Lockdown. The world has stopped. We are
planeless, boatless, trainless.
Silence. Bliss. Loneliness? For some.
Finally, unadulterated, unaltered, unsullied,
whale songs echo underwater once more

Scientists listen in silence, marvel, awe,
as inside whales' heads, air cycles in red sacs
reverberates, resounds. Bony scaffold,
cartilage, space, all now song creators,
cetacean songs, singing the shape of oceans
call to each other, call to us

After centuries of slaughter, now
we love them so much. Too much.
Whale as new age spiritual totem,
grist for would-be eco-warriors.

Or tourist tick box, whereby
we watched them by the noisy boatload,
we humans changed whale symphonies, unknowing, unwitting.
They called louder, called less.
We muted love songs, location echoes,
childcare tunes, wayfinding melodies.
They call louder, call less…

Cyclic motifs of exploitation, destruction
repeat, echo, rebound across shared planet
generations plundered, killed, burned, squandered…
…everything…
Perceived progress, wealth, ease…
sowed the seeds of our destruction until
this cycle, mighty whale-sized, whole-world-sized cycle,
now witnesses dog days, plague days, end days

Calling louder, calling less, whale weaves a story
up and down the world-staves, across time
pursued, hunted, exploited, endangered,
whales breached through our petty wars and revolutions
survived to witness whale wilderness wiped out,
noise-invaded, plastic-polluted, climate-warmed

Call louder, call less, call the children,
wish for whales to cruise forever
majestic, attuned, unfettered.

Covid #3

Newman, Australia, 2021, 23.3575° S, 119.7303° E
John's great-great-great-great-grandson

…[the whale]…sang to the world a wonderful song
of shimmering ice and coral caves…
and said to the snail, come sail with me.
– Donaldson & Scheffler

This author reads aloud,
of the snail and the whale
and wonders, darling,
will you ever see the whales?

References

Texts
Aberdeen Free Press. (1893). *The SS Eclipse*
Coleridge, Samuel Taylor. *The Rime of the Ancient Mariner*. First published 1798
Duncan, A. (2019). *Shetland and the Whaling*. The Shetland Times, Lerwick
Giggs, R. (2020). *Fathoms*. Scribe, Melbourne
Grassic-Gibbon, L. (1946). *A Scots Quair*. Jarrolds, London
Lopez, B. (1998). *Arctic Dreams*. Harvill Press, London
Scheffler, A., & J. Donaldson (2016). *The Snail and the Whale*. Pan Macmillan, London

Electronic
Aldred, J. https://chinadialogueocean.net/en/conservation/13512-priceless-poo-the-global-cooling-effect-of-whales/
http://www.mcjazz.f2s.com/WhalerLife.htm
https://en.wikipedia.org/wiki/Bowhead_whale
https://www.cliftonhotelpeterhead.co.uk/
https://www.findmypast.com.au/
https://media.scotslanguage.com/library/document/RGU_Doric_Dictionary.pdf
https://www.scottish-places.info
https://www.theguardian.com/environment/2020/apr/27/silence-is-golden-for-whales-as-lockdown-reduces-ocean-noise-coronavirus
https://www.whalingmuseum.org/learn/research-topics/whaling-history/

Images
p 19. Whaling crew at Peterhead, Scotland, about 1881. Image courtesy of Historic Environment Scotland

p 21. SS *Eclipse* at Dundee Docks, Scotland. Image courtesy of Historic Environment Scotland

p 23. Whaling log. Image courtesy of Historic Environment Scotland

p 26. Map of Greenland showing whaling grounds. Emanuel Bowen (c. 1694–1767). https://commons.wikimedia.org/wiki/File:Old_Greenland_1747.jpg

p 37. Bowhead whale drawing. Michelson, M. 2015. California Academy of Sciences.
https://www.calacademy.org/explore-science/ bowhead-longevity

p 44. Rainbow Warrior. Image courtesy of Greenpeace. www.photo.greenpeace.org

www.ingramcontent.com/pod-product-compliance
Lightning Source LLC
Chambersburg PA
CBHW070339120526
44590CB00017B/2945